In the name of God

Hamburger paragraphs

Dr Azadeh Nemati

سرشناسه: نعمتی، آزاده، ۱۳۵۴ –
عنوان و نام پدیدآور: Hamburger paragraph / Azadeh Nemati
مشخصات نشر: شیراز :کوشا مهر ، ۱۳۹۶=۲۰۱۷ م.
مشخصات ظاهری: ۶۷ ص.: مصور (رنگی).
شابک: ۹۷۸-۹۶۴-۹۷۴-۲۱۲-۰
وضعیت فهرست نویسی: فیپا
یادداشت: انگلیسی
آوانویسی عنوان: همبرگر پاراگرافز.
موضوع: زبان انگلیسی--پاراگراف--راهنمای آموزشی
English Language--Paragraphs--Study and teaching
موضوع: زبان انگلیسی--پاراگراف--مسائل، تمرین ها و غیره
English Language--Paragraphs--Problems, exercises, etc
رده بندی کنگره: ۱۳۹۶ ۸ هـ ۷ ن/ ۱۴۳۹ PE
رده بندی دیویی: ۸۰۸/۰۴۲
شماره کتابشناسی ملی: ۴۸۲۱۶۴۷

Hamburger paragraph

مؤلف: دکتر آزاده نعمتی

ناشر: انتشارات کوشا مهر، نوبت چاپ: اول ۱۳۹۶

انتشارات کوشا مهر

مرکز نشر و پخش کتابهای دانشگاهی

شیراز – بولوار کریم خان زند – روبروی خیام- پاساژ مسعودی- پلاک ۳۳

تلفن: ۳۲۳۰۳۷۹۸ دورنگار: ۳۲۳۵۸۴۶۵

ناشر برگزیده سالهای ۷۴، ۷۶، ۷۹، ۸۰، ۸۱

خادم نشر سال ۷۷ و ۸۳

Chapter one: How to write a really great paragraph!

The Topic Sentence (Top Bun) 10

The First Detail (Lettuce)..................................11

The Second Detail (Tomato) 12

The Third Detail (Cheese)..............................13

The Last Detail (Meat) 13

The Closing Sentence (Bottom Bun) 15

Chapter two: Writing Paragraphs

Warm-Up 18

Paragraphs 18

Paragraphs: A Bad Example 18

Paragraph Structure 19

Practicing with Paragraphs 20

Topic Sentences 20

Topic Sentences: Good Examples 20

Topic Sentences: Bad Examples 21

Practice with Topic Sentences 21

Chapter three: What Makes a Good Paragraph?

3 Things Make a Good Paragraph: 24

Let's Start with Unity 24

LET'S SEE AN EXAMPLE 25

#2: COHERENCE 26

"How can we create coherence?" 26

2nd Way to Create Coherence: Transitional Words 28

"We want to see a connection!" 28

3: Elaboration 28

Here are are Nine Ways to Elaborate! 28

Chapter four: How to Write a Paragraph Or How to Build a Big Mac

Big Mac Cheeseburger 32

A good paragraph is like a Big Mac. 32

The top bun of a paragraph is a topic sentence. 32

The topic sentence introduces the main idea of a paragraph. 32

Would you like a cheeseburger without a topbun? 33

What's missing? 33

Chapter five: The Five-Paragraph Essay

A Framework for Expository Writing................37

Different Kinds of Writing..................................38

Expository Writing...38

Expository Writing Uses Transitions.................38

So, your teacher gives you a prompt and tells you to write an expository essay:....................39

It's Easy!..39

Use Correct Paragraph Form............................40

The Beginning -Your First Sentences 40

Now end with a conclusion:.............................40

You already have your first paragraph done! Pretty easy, huh?..41

Paragraph 1: The Introduction.........................41

Paragraph 1: Example 42

Paragraph 3: Example #1 42

Paragraph 3: Example #2 43

Paragraph 4: Example #3 44

Paragraph 5: Conclusion 44

There you have it! 45

Chapter six: How to Write a Good Paragraph: A Step-by-Step Guide

Step 1: Decide the Topic of Your Paragraph ...50

Step 2: Develop a Topic Sentence 51

Step 3: Demonstrate Your Point.......................52

Step 4: Give Your Paragraph Meaning 53

Step 5: Conclude..54

Step 6: Look Over and Proofread 55

Chapter seven: PROOFREADING & EDITING STRATEGIES

Take a break. 58

Read out loud. 58

Involve others...59

Run Spell Check. 59

Make MS Word read your paper back to you. 59

Check your paper using our Revision Checklist..60

Bibliography 63

Chapter one

How to write a really great paragraph!

10 :: Hamburger paragraphs

The Topic Sentence (Top Bun)

- Very first sentence of your paragraph.
- <u>Always</u> needs to be indented.
- Tells what your paragraph is going to be about.

There are many reasons that I love to teach. First of all, I love to teach because I love being at school. Another reason I love teachin g is that the days go by quickly. A third reason I love to teach is because I love seeing a student understand something new. Finally, I love to teach because I love to be around kids. These are just a few reasons I love to teach.

The First Detail (Lettuce)

- Should **not** be the most important detail.
- Needs to follow directly after the topic sentence.
- Needs to be full of good "lettucy" details!

There are many reasons that I love to teach. **First of all, I love to teach because I love being at school**. Another reason I love teaching is that the days go by quickly. A third reason I love to teach is because I love seeing a student understand something new. Finally, I love to teach because I love to be around kids. These are just a few reasons I love to teach.

The Second Detail (Tomato)

- Still should **not** be the most important detail.
- Needs to follow directly after the lettuce sentence.
- Needs to be full of good "juicy" details!

There are many reasons that I love to teach. First of all, I love to teach because I love being at school. **Another reason I love teaching is that the days go by quickly**. A third reason I love to teach is because I love seeing a student understand something new. Finally, I love to teach because I love to be around kids. These are just a few reasons I love to teach.

Chapter one: How to write a really great ... :: 13

The Third Detail (Cheese)

- Still **not** be the most important detail.
- Needs to start differently than other sentences.
- Needs to be full of good "cheesy" details!

There are many reasons that I love to teach. First of all, I love to teach because I love being at school. Another reason I love teaching is that the days go by quickly. **A third reason I love to teach is because I love seeing a student understand something new**. Finally, I love to teach because I love to be around kids. These are just a few reasons I love to teach.

14 :: Hamburger paragraphs

The Last Detail (Meat)

- **Finally!! The most important detail.**
- **Should start differently than most of the other sentences.**
- **Needs to be full of good "meaty" details!**

There are many reasons that I love to teach. First of all, I love to teach because I love being at school. Another reason I love teaching is that the days go by quickly. A third reason I love to teach is because I love seeing a student understand something new. **Finally, I love to teach because I love to be around kids**. These are just a few reasons I love to teach.

The Closing Sentence (Bottom Bun)

- Should look a lot like the topic sentence.
- Needs to summarize the topic.
- **Needs to be an obvious end to the sentence.**

There are many reasons that I love to teach. First of all, I love to teach because I love being at school. Another reason I love teaching is that the days go by quickly. A third reason I love to teach is because I love seeing a student understand something new. Finally, I love to teach because I love to be around kids. **These are just a few reasons I love to teach.**

16 :: Hamburger paragraphs

Topic Sentence ....
....

Detail # 1 ....
....

Detail # 2 ....
....

Detail # 3 ....
....

Concluding Sentence ....
....

Chapter two
Writing Paragraphs

18 :: Hamburger paragraphs

Warm-Up

- One partner closes his/her eyes.
- The other partner chooses an object.
- Describe the object to the other person WITHOUT mentioning the name of the object.
- The person with eyes closed can only say, "I need more details!" until they can guess what the object is.

Paragraphs

- What is a paragraph?
- A paragraph is a group of sentences that develops an idea.
- The first sentence of a paragraph should be indented.
- The sentences in the paragraph support and give examples of the main idea.

Paragraphs: A Bad Example

I live in a house in west Provo. I like the view from our house. We have lived there since November. We also have a car that I like very much. We were in an accident a few months ago. We hit a deer

that was crossing the street at night. I felt sorry for the deer, but it cost a lot of money to repair the car.

My husband and I bought our first house last November, and we love it. It is located in west Provo near Utah Lake. Although we cannot see the lake from our house, we do have a beautiful view of Mount Timpanogos. Our house has three bedrooms, two bathrooms, a living room and a family room, and a large kitchen and dining area. We also have a large backyard and a small garden. We are very happy to own our own home, and I hope that we will live there for several years.

Paragraph Structure

- A paragraph should have a logical structure that is easy to put into an outline:

  I. Topic Sentence

  II. Supporting Detail

  III. Supporting Detail

  IV. Supporting Detail

  V. Concluding Sentence

Practicing with Paragraphs

- Find one of your warm-up writings in your notebook.
- Choose one idea from your writing and create an outline for a well-structured paragraph using this idea.
- Write the paragraph.

Topic Sentences

- A topic sentence is the sentence that tells the reader the main idea of the paragraph.
- The topic sentence should contain only one main idea. It should be specific and detailed.
- The topic sentence is often found at the beginning of the paragraph, but it can be in other places, too.

Topic Sentences: Good Examples

- When I was a child, I lived in a house that had a strange atmosphere.
- There is a canyon in Northern Arizona that is the most beautiful place on Earth.

- My favorite item of clothing is a comfortable, worn pair of jeans that I have had for many years.

Topic Sentences: Bad Examples

- I went to the Grand Canyon this winter and to Mexico in the spring of 1994.
- My friend is nice.
- I like my bedroom.

Practice with Topic Sentences

- Write a topic sentence for each of the following topics:

    A) your favorite possession

    B) an interesting person you know

    C) a beautiful place

22 :: Hamburger paragraphs

Topic Sentence ....
....

Detail # 1 ....
....

Detail # 2 ....
....

Detail # 3 ....
....

Concluding Sentence ....
....

Chapter three

What Makes a Good Paragraph?

24 :: Hamburger paragraphs

"We have to be able to understand it!"

"What can we do to make our reader understand our writing?"

3 Things Make a Good Paragraph:

1. Unity
2. Coherence
3. Elaboration

"What do all of these mean?"

Let's Start with Unity…

"What does unity mean to you?"

- When a paragraph has unity, all the sentences relate directly to the main idea.

Chapter three: What Makes a God paragraph? :: 25

- If there is a sentence off topic at all, this begins to create confusion for your reader.

Use only the most

LET'S SEE AN EXAMPLE...

Find the sentence in the paragraph that <u>destroys the unity</u> and doesn't belong.

Hamburger paragraphs

The disappearance of Amealia Earhart remains a mystery. Earhart, who was the first woman pilot to fly across the Atlantic Ocean, crashed into the Pacific Ocean while attempting to fly around the world. She was born in Atchison, Kansas, in 1897. Some researchers believe that she survived the crash into the Pacific, because radio distress calls were received. An intensive search for the source of the signals was made. Searchers were not able to find her, however. Finally, the distress signals ceased. In spite of continued searches by airplane and ship, no clue about what became of Amelia Earhart has yet been found.

#2: COHERENCE

- A coherent paragraph is one in which all of the sentences _logically fit together_.
- When a paragraph has coherence, your reader can easily see how all of the _details are connected_.

"How can we create coherence?"

There are 2 ways!

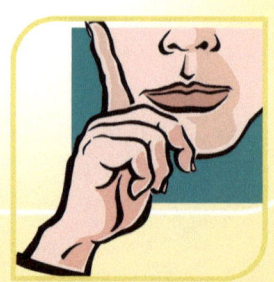

Chapter three: What Makes a God paragraph? 27

1. Order details in a way that makes sense.
2. Show a connection by using transitional words.

"Order Please!"

Not that kind of order!

Organizing your details in a specific order is 1 way to make your paragraph clear and coherent.

Chronological Order	Presents details in the order they occur
Spatial Order	Presents details according to location
Order of Importance	Details are least important to most <u>or</u> the reverse
Logical Order	Groups related details together

"Look at the chart!"

2nd Way to Create Coherence: Transitional Words

"We want to see a connection!"

Transitional words help the reader <u>see *a relationship*</u> between ideas.

After   finally   soon   later   meanwhile
first   next   before   then

They <u>*tie things together*</u>!

across   beyond   under   around   inside
down   because   therefore   consequently

3: Elaboration

"Give us more detail!

Elaboration means: to *add more detail,* so your reader can get a clear picture of what you mean!

Here are are Nine Ways to Elaborate!

Use *Highly Descriptive Words*: vivid adj.'s & adv.'s, precise V's & N's.

2. Give a detailed *Definition* of the subject or detail.

3. Provide an *Example* that shows your point.

Chapter three: What Makes a God paragraph? :: 29

4. Use <u>Comparison</u>: Similes and/or Metaphors.

5. Use <u>Contrast</u> to show how your idea is different from something else.

6. Include a <u>Fact</u> to support your main idea.

7. Use a <u>Statistic</u> (a fact in numerical form) to support your main idea.

8. Use <u>Sensory Details</u> that appeals to one or more of the 5 senses.

9. Use <u>Cause & Effect</u> to explain how 1 thing causes another.

"Now we see what you're talking about!"

30 :: Hamburger paragraphs

Topic Sentence ....
....

Detail # 1 ....

Detail # 2 ....

Detail # 3 ....

Concluding Sentence ....
....

Chapter four

How to Write a Paragraph Or How to Build a Big Mac

32 :: Hamburger paragraphs

Big Mac Cheeseburger

What are the ingredients of a Big Mac Cheeseburger?

- Top Bun
- Lettuce
- Tomato
- Cheese
- Onion
- Special Sauce
- Hamburger
- Bottom Bun

A good paragraph is like a Big Mac.

- The top and bottom bun hold the stuff inside together.

The top bun of a paragraph is a topic sentence.

The topic sentence introduces the main idea of a paragraph.

- Although most people believe that man's best friend is a dog, I think it should be a cat.
- Cats have been used as pets since the time of the pharaohs in Egypt. They have been found in

countries all over the world. Obviously, cats have been the favorites of man for hundreds of years. I suppose cats are so well liked because they are gentle, friendly and easy to take care of.

Would you like a cheeseburger without a top bun?

A paragraph without a topic sentence is like warm milk –you don't know if you want to swallow it.

A topic sentence is like a . . .

- A ship without its rudder.
- An army without its general.
- A vacation trip without a map.

What's missing?

- He collects books that were written over a hundred years ago. But he is also interested in the best sellers of today. If I ever need to get him a present, I know I can always please him by buying him a book.

34 :: Hamburger paragraphs

- The most beautiful flower is the rose because it comes in so many different colors. Another beautiful flower is the daisy which sometimes grows wild. Spring flowers like tulips, daffodils, and crocuses are also very pretty.
- First, Canada has an excellent health care system. All Canadians have access to medical services at a reasonable price. Second, Canada has a high standard of education. Finally, Canada's cities are clean and efficiently managed.

The most beautiful flower is the rose because it comes in so many different colors. Another beautiful flower is the daisy which sometimes grows wild. Spring flowers like tulips, daffodils, and crocuses are also very pretty.

- Which of the following topic sentences is the best one for the above paragraph?
- A. Don't you just love spring?
- B. The rose is the most loved flower the world over.
- C. There are many lovely flowers to consider for your garden.

First, Canada has an excellent health care system. All Canadians have access to medical services at a reasonable price. Second, Canada has a high standard of education. Finally, Canada's cities are clean and efficiently managed

- A. Canada is our friendly neighbor to the north.
- B. There are three reasons why Canada is one of the best countries of the world.
- C. Choose Canada as a great place to vacation.

36 :: Hamburger paragraphs

Topic Sentence ....
....

Detail # 1 ....
....

Detail # 2 ....
....

Detail # 3 ....
....

Concluding Sentence ....
....

Chapter five

The Five-Paragraph Essay A Framework for Expository Writing

Different Kinds of Writing

- We write for fun. We write letters, stories, jokes, and to share information with our family or friends.

- Most school writing, however, is *expository writing* and fits into a different category.

The purpose of most expository writing is to communicate ideas or answer questions.

Expository Writing

- Gives information about a topic
- Explains ideas
- Gives directions
- Shows how to do something

Expository Writing Uses Transitions

Writer's Express says:

"Expository writing uses transition words (such as first, second, and most importantly). These words help guide the reader through the explanation."

Writer's Express - A Handbook for Young Writers, Thinkers, and Learners ©1995

So, your teacher gives you a prompt and tells you to write an expository essay:

"Write about your favorite pet."

What do you do???

Don't panic.

Follow this plan…

(Watch for the color-coding, it will help you organize your ideas.)

It's Easy!

Start with your main idea or topic.

(use key words from the prompt)

You ONLY Need *Three* Ideas…

- Three reasons that show your topic sentence is true
- And three examples for each of your reasons (Remember to <u>show</u>, not tell.)

That's all you need for the start of a great essay!!!

40 :: Hamburger paragraphs

Use Correct Paragraph Form

Each paragraph must include:
- Topic Sentence
- Three Examples
- Conclusion
- No paragraph should be less
- than five sentences.

The Beginning -Your First Sentences

Start with a topic sentence that uses the *key words* from the prompt. Then write *three reasons* that prove the topic sentence is true.

My favorite pet is my dog, Romeo. He is a beautiful and easy to care for. Playing with him is lots of fun. He always takes care of me.

Now end with a conclusion:

Remember, each paragraph must have a concluding sentence.

Finish with a sentence that restates your topic sentence "My favorite pet is my dog, Romeo." using different words.

I have never had a better pet.

You already have your first paragraph done! Pretty easy, huh?

To make it even easier look at this organizational plan using color-coding.

Paragraph 1: The Introduction

- Introduction or Topic Sentence (Use key words from the prompt)
- First Subtopic (A "Showing" Example)
- Second Subtopic (A "Showing" Example)
- Third Subtopic (A "Showing" Example)
- Conclusion (Restates Introduction)

Paragraph 1: Example

My favorite pet is my dog, Romeo. He is beautiful and easy to care for. Playing with him is lots of fun. He always takes care of me. I have never had a better pet.

Restate each subtopic as the topic sentence for each of the next three paragraphs.

First Subtopic (Example #1)

"He is beautiful and easy to care for." is the topic sentence you will restate for your next paragraph.

Paragraph 3: Example #1

- Topic Sentence (Restates Example #1 from the Introduction "He is beautiful and easy to care for.")

- 3 Example Sentences (Prove your Topic Sentence)

- Concluding Sentence (Restates Topic Sentence from Example #1)

Romeo is beautiful and easy to care for. He is a tricolor Sheltie, mostly black with white and a bit of brown. Caring for him is easy because I simply have to make sure he has fresh water and food every day. I exercise him by throwing his toys.

Because he is good looking and doesn't require much care Romeo is a good pet.

Restate the second subtopic as the topic sentence for the next paragraph.

Second Subtopic (Example #2)

"Playing with him is lots of fun." is the topic sentence you will restate for your next paragraph.

Paragraph 3: Example #2

• Topic Sentence (Restate Example #2 from the Introduction "Playing with him is lots of fun.")

• 3 Example Sentences (Prove your Topic Sentence)

• Concluding Sentence (Restates Topic Sentence from Example #2)

Use the third subtopic (example) as the topic sentence for the next paragraph.

Third Subtopic (Example #3)

"He always takes care of me."

 is the topic sentence for your next paragraph.

44 :: Hamburger paragraphs

Paragraph 4: Example #3

- Topic Sentence (Restates Example #3 from the Introduction "Romeo takes care of me.")
- 3 Example Sentences (That prove your Topic Sentence)
- Concluding Sentence (Restates Topic Sentence from Example #3)

Romeo takes care of me. He always follows me when I leave a room. When I am sitting on a couch he plops down right beside me. On sunny days when we are hiking in the woods he always makes sure that I keep up with the rest of the family. He always watches out for me.

Paragraph 5: Conclusion

(Restates Paragraph 1: Introduction)

- Introduction
- First Subtopic (Example)
- Second Subtopic (Example)
- Third Sentence (Example)
- Conclusion

As you can see, Romeo is a great pet. I am proud of him and he doesn't require much care. Playing with him is very pleasurable. I am always safe because he watches over me. Romeo is a wonderful pet.

There you have it!

Expository writing isn't that difficult when you have *a plan*. To make it even easier you may want to use a graphic organizer like the following ones to organize your thoughts.

46 :: Hamburger paragraphs

Five-Paragraph Essay Organizer

Name _____

- Main Idea
- Main Example 2
  - Example 1
  - Example 2
  - Example 3
- Main Example 1
  - Example 1
  - Example 2
  - Example 3
- Main Example 2
  - Example 1
  - Example 2
  - Example 3

Have fun with your writing & remember, you only need *THREE IDEAS* for a great expository essay!

48 :: Hamburger paragraphs

Topic Sentence ....
....

Detail # 1 ....
....

Detail # 2 ....
....

Detail # 3 ....
....

Concluding Sentence ....
....

Chapter six

How to Write a Good Paragraph: A Step-by-Step Guide

Writing well composed academic paragraphs can be tricky. The following is a guide on how to draft, expand, refine, and explain your ideas so that you write *clear*, *well-developed* paragraphs and discussion posts:

Step 1: Decide the Topic of Your Paragraph

Before you can begin writing, you need to know what you are writing about. First, look at the writing prompt or assignment topic. As you look at the prompt, note any key terms or repeated phrases because you will want to use those words in your response. Then ask yourself:

• On what topic am I supposed to be writing?

• What do I know about this topic already?

• If I don't know how to respond to this assignment, where can I go to find some answers?

• What does this assignment mean to me? How do I relate to it?

After looking at the prompt and doing some additional reading and research, you should better understand your topic and what you need to discuss.

Step 2: Develop a Topic Sentence

Before writing a paragraph, it is important to think first about the **topic** and then what you want to say about the topic. Most often, the topic is easy, but the question then turns to *what* you want to say about the topic. This concept is sometimes called the **controlling idea.**

Strong paragraphs are typically about one main idea or topic, which is often explicitly stated in a **topic sentence**. Good **topic sentences** should always contain both (1) a **topic** and (2) a **controlling idea**.

The **topic** – The main subject matter or idea covered in the paragraph.

The **controlling idea** – This idea focuses the topic by providing direction to the composition.

Read the following topic sentences. They all contain a **topic** (in orange) and a **controlling idea** (in purple). When your paragraphs contain a clearly stated **topic sentence** such as one of the following, your reader will know what to expect and, therefore, understand your ideas better.

Examples of **topic sentences**:

• People can avoid **plagiarizing by taking certain precautions**.

• There are **several advantages to online education**.

• **Effective leadership** requires **specific qualities that anyone can develop**.

Step 3: Demonstrate Your Point

After stating your topic sentence, you need to provide information to prove, illustrate, clarify, and/or exemplify your point.

Ask yourself:

• What examples can I use to support my point?

• What information can I provide to help clarify my thoughts?

• How can I support my point with specific data, experiences, or other factual material?

• What information does the reader need to know in order to see my point?

Here is a list of the kinds of information you can add to your paragraph:

Proprietary Information of Ashford University, Created by Academics, CR 215140

- Facts, details, reasons, examples
- Information from the readings or class discussions
- Paraphrases or short quotations
- Statistics, polls, percentages, data from research studies
- Personal experience, stories, anecdotes, examples from your life

Sometimes, adding transitional or introductory phrases like: *for example, for instance, first, second,* or *last* can help guide the reader. Also, make sure you are citing your sources appropriately.

Step 4: Give Your Paragraph Meaning

After you have given the reader enough information to see and understand your point, you need to explain why this information is relevant, meaningful, or interesting.

Ask yourself:

• What does the provided information mean?

• How does it relate to your overall point, argument, or thesis?

• Why is this information important/ significant/ meaningful?

• How does this information relate to the assignment or course I am taking?

Step 5: Conclude

After illustrating your point with relevant information, add a **concluding sentence.** Concluding sentences link one paragraph to the next and provide another device for helping you ensure your paragraph is unified. While not all paragraphs include a concluding sentence, you should always consider whether one is appropriate. Concluding sentences have *two* crucial roles in paragraph writing:

First, they draw together the information you have presented to elaborate your controlling idea by:

• Summarizing the point(s) you have made.

- Repeating words or phrases from the topic sentence.
- Using linking words that indicate that conclusions are being drawn (e.g., therefore, thus, resulting).

Second, they often link the current paragraph to the following paragraph. They may anticipate the topic sentence of the next paragraph by:

- Introducing a word/phrase or new concept which will then be picked up in the topic sentence of the next paragraph.
- Using words or phrases that point ahead (e.g., the following, another, other).

Step 6: Look Over and Proofread

The last step in good paragraph writing is proofreading and revision. Before you submit your writing, look over your work at least one more time. Try reading your paragraph out loud to make sure it makes sense. Also, ask yourself these questions:

- Does my paragraph answer the prompt and support my thesis?
- Does it make sense? Does it use the appropriate academic voice?

View additional proofreading tips and editing strategies.

 Chapter six: How to Write a Good paragraph ... 57

Topic Sentence ....
....

Detail # 1 ....
....

Detail # 2 ....
....

Detail # 3 ....
....

Concluding Sentence ....
....

Chapter seven
PROOFREADING & EDITING STRATEGIES

Many students do not realize that proofreading and editing are the final stages of the writing process. Every assignment—a discussion board post, essay, proposal, etc., should be proofread and edited before submitting it to the instructor. To guide you in this process, here are some proofreading and editing strategies that work well:

Take a break.

Allow yourself some time between writing and proofreading. Even a five-minute break can be productive because it will allow you some distance from what you have written, so you can return to your paper with a fresh eye and mind.

Read out loud.

Reading what you wrote out loud to yourself can help you catch both grammatical errors and awkward organization or development of ideas.

Involve others.

Asking a friend or family member to read your paper will give you another perspective on your writing. Also, a fresh reader will be able to help you catch mistakes that you might have overlooked.

Run Spell Check.

The Spell Check function in Microsoft Word can help you quickly find the spelling and grammar mistakes in the Word document. To run Spell Check, click on the Spelling & Grammar button in the "Review" tab of Microsoft Word. Or, if you notice Microsoft is underlining your words in red, green, or blue, simply right click on those words and Microsoft will offer your suggestions on how to correct the issue.

Make MS Word read your paper back to you.

Did you know that Microsoft Word can read your paper out loud to you? By using the Speak feature

in MS Word, or the Text to Speech feature for Macs, your computer can read your paper to you, allowing you to listen for awkward or confusing sentences.

Check your paper using our Revision Checklist.

To make sure you have done a thorough writing your paper, review it using our Revision Checklist. If you can check off all of the boxes, you are well on your way to a solid paper.

Main Components

Prompt:
- ☐ Did you follow *all* of the assignment instructions?

Hook:
- ☐ Do your opening sentences draw your reader in?

Introduction:
- ☐ Does your introduction introduce your topic to the reader?
- ☐ Does your introduction define your topic?
- ☐ Does your introduction give some idea of where your paper is going?
- ☐ Does your introduction lead your reader clearly to your thesis?

Get more help with Introductions.

Thesis Statement:
- ☐ Is your thesis specific and focused?
- ☐ Does it detail what the reader can expect from the rest of the paper?
- ☐ Does your thesis make a point worth considering? Does it answer the questions, "So what? Who cares?"
- ☐ Does your thesis contain the point you are trying to make and the reasons for thinking/feeling this way?

Get more help with Thesis Statements.

Topic Sentences:
- ☐ Do your paragraphs begin with topic sentences that summarize the main idea of the paragraph and state what the paragraph will be about?

Avoid beginning body paragraphs with quotes or facts.

Body Paragraphs:
- ☐ Does each paragraph have a single topic or point?
- ☐ Do you develop your claims thoroughly with evidence, reasons, or examples?
- ☐ Do all of the ideas in the paragraph flow together and prove or illustrate your topic sentence?
- ☐ Have you made adequate transitions from paragraph to paragraph?
- ☐ Is each paragraph related to your main idea or thesis?

Get for more information about writing good paragraphs.

Conclusion Paragraph:
- ☐ Does your conclusion sum up your main points?
- ☐ Does your conclusion reflect on the importance of your topic or main idea?
- ☐ Does your conclusion leave your reader with something to think about?

Get more help with conclusions.

Citations

Direction Quotations:
- ☐ Did you introduce your quotes? Who said it? When? In what?
- ☐ Do your quotes have quotation marks around them?
- ☐ Have you explained your quotes and their importance to the point you are trying to make?
- ☐ Did you cite your quotations using in-text citations?
- ☐ Do your in-text citations contain the author's last name, the year the resource was published, and the page or paragraph number where the quote was found?

For example:
⇒ According to LastName (year), "quote" (p.#).
⇒ As LastName (year) states "quote" (p.#).
⇒ "Quote" (LastName, Year, p.#).

Paraphrasing & Summarizing:
- ☐ Did you cite the information you paraphrased or summarized with in-text citations?

For example:
⇒ According to LastName (year), paraphrased information goes here.
⇒ Summary goes here (LastName, Year).

Click the following links for more information about quoting, paraphrasing, and summarizing.

Voice & Style

- ☐ Did you avoid using overly casual language or jargon?
- ☐ Does your paper sound appropriately academic?
- ☐ Are your sentences clear, precise, and easy to understand?
- ☐ Do your ideas flow logically from one idea to the next?

Format

- ☐ Is your paper formatted according to APA (6th Edition) guidelines?
- ☐ Do you have a title page and headers?
- ☐ Do you have a References list that cites all sources used?
- ☐ Did you use 12 pt. Times New Roman font?

Get help with formatting your paper

Proofreading

- ☐ Did you proofread your paper for spelling and grammatical errors?
- ☐ Did you run your paper through Grammarly?

62 :: Hamburger paragraphs

Topic Sentence ....
....

Detail # 1 ....
....

Detail # 2 ....
....

Detail # 3 ....
....

Concluding Sentence ....
....

Bibliography

Chapter One

Hamburger Paragraphs. Retrieved on 10 of January 14, 2017 from

www.readingrockets.org/content/pdfs/parahamburger.ppt

Chapter Two

Writing Paragraphs by Tarasine A. Buck . Retrieved on 18 of January, 2017 from

www.banarvan.com/DynamicContent/UsersDirectory/admin/.../1%20paragraphs.ppt

Chapter Three

What Makes a Good Paragraph? Retrieved on 14 of March, 2016 from

www.stcs.k12.oh.us/Downloads/Paragraph%20Lesson.ppt.

Chapter Four

How to Write a Paragraph? Retrieved on 25 of April, 2016 from

www.nebo.edu/learning_resources/ppt/6-12/write_paragraph.ppt.

Chapter Five

The Five-Paragraph Essay. Retrieved on 17 of April, 2016 from

www.banarvan.com/DynamicContent/UsersDirectory/.../five-paragraph%20essay.ppt

Chapter Six

How to Write a Good Paragraph: A Step-by-Step Guide. Retrieved on 17 of January, 2017 from

https://awc.ashford.edu/PDFHandouts%5CHow%20to%20Write%20a%20Good%20P...

Chapter Seven

Proofreading and editing strategies. Retrieved on 17 of January, 2017 from

https://awc.ashford.edu/PDFHandouts%5CHow%20to%20Write%20a%20Good%20P...

◻ به همین قلم ◻

ترجمه:

- آموزش کودک
- ارزیابی تفکر انتقادی و خلاق
- فرهنگ اصطلاحات پرستاری

تالیف:

- Principles of writing resume (Persian Edition).
  اصول رزومه نویسی
- Samples of simple text translation.
  نمونه‌های ترجمه متون ساده
- English-Persian Dictionary of animal Idioms.
  فرهنگ اصطلاحات حیوانات
- English-Persian Dictionary of color Idioms.
  فرهنگ اصطلاحات رنگ ها
- English-Persian Dictionary of body Idioms.
  فرهنگ اصطلاحات اعضای بدن
- English through games (Persian edition).
  آموزش زبان انگلیسی از طریق بازی

- Easy reading based on concordle-cloud.
- How to write a research proposal, paper or thesis.

- A collection of practical questionnaires for ELT researchers.
- Aspects of Language Learning Strategies (LLS): Focus on vocabulary learning strategies (VLS).
- Paper submission guidelines in ISI indexed journals (Persian Edition).
- Special English for the students of midwifery.
- Phonetic reader.
- Special English for the students of biology.
- Skills: How to be a better student and language learner by learning techniques
- The Impact of Vocabulary Strategies on Short and long Term. Germany: LAP LAMBERT Academic Publishing.
- Tear and tea (2010). UK: Xlibriss.
- A span between the moon and me. Ireland: Lapwing publications.

☐ ارتباط با نویسنده از طریق سایت www.banarvan.com ☐

www.ingramcontent.com/pod-product-compliance
Lightning Source LLC
Chambersburg PA
CBHW041623220426
43662CB00001B/30